D1370599

# Penguins

Diane Swanson

**Gareth Stevens**
Publishing

**Please visit our web site at: www.garethstevens.com**
**For a free color catalog describing Gareth Stevens Publishing's list of high-quality books**
**and multimedia programs, call 1-800-542-2595 (USA) or 1-800-387-3178 (Canada).**
**Gareth Stevens Publishing's fax: 1-877-542-2596.**

The publishers acknowledge the support of the Canada Council for the Arts and the Cultural Services
Branch of the Government of British Columbia in making this publication possible.

**Library of Congress Cataloging-in-Publication Data**

Swanson, Diane, 1944-
    Penguins / by Diane Swanson.
       p. cm. — (Welcome to the world of animals)
    Includes index.
    Summary: Introduces the physical characteristics, behavior, and habitat of various
kinds of penguins.
      ISBN-10: 0-8368-4025-9   ISBN-13: 978-0-8368-4025-4 (lib. bdg.)
      1. Penguins—Juvenile literature. [1. Penguins.] I. Title.
QL696.S473S94   2004
598.47—dc22                            2003061789

This edition first published in 2004 by
**Gareth Stevens Publishing**
A Weekly Reader® Company
1 Reader's Digest Road
Pleasantville, NY 10570-7000 USA

This U.S. edition © 2004 by Gareth Stevens, Inc. Original edition © 2003 by Diane Swanson.
First published in 2003 by Whitecap Books, Vancouver, as *Welcome to the Whole World of Penguins*
in the *Welcome to the Whole World of Animals* series. Additional end matter © 2004
by Gareth Stevens, Inc.

Series editor: Betsy Rasmussen
Design: Melissa Valuch
Cover design: Steve Penner

Cover photograph: Wayne Lynch
Photo credits: Wayne Lynch 4, 14, 16, 24, 26, 30; Joe Sroka/Dembinsky Photo Assoc. 6; John
Gerlach/Dembinsky Photo Assoc. 8; Hal Beral/aaaimagemakers.com 10; Peter Oxford/Nature
Picture Library 12; Mark J. Thomas/Dembinsky Photo Assoc. 18; Lynn M. Stone 20, 22; Fritz
Polking/Dembinsky Photo Assoc. 28

Printed in the United States of America

2 3 4 5 6 7 8 9 10 10 09

# Contents

# World of Difference

Penguins fly through water, not air. Unlike most other birds, penguins have no flight feathers and no true wings. Instead, they have stiff, narrow flippers designed for fast swimming.

On land and on ice, penguins waddle along on short legs and webbed feet. Sharp claws help them grip, but the birds may trip over rocks and knobs of ice.

Some penguins walk just a little; others walk a lot. Adélie (uh-DAY-lee) penguins might travel 60 miles (100 kilometers) to reach water, walking as fast as people do —about 3 miles (5 kilometers) per hour.

**Sw-o-o-sh! Adélie penguins toboggan on their bellies.**

5

When penguins are in a hurry to cross a stretch of ice, they s-l-i-d-e on their tummies. They push off with their feet, often paddling and balancing with their flippers. Some kinds of penguins can toboggan faster than people can ski over a level surface of land.

**Earth's smallest kind of penguin is named "little penguin."**

Of the world's seventeen kinds of penguins, the biggest are the emperor penguins. They stand about 4 feet (1.2 meters) tall. The smallest kind are called little, blue, or fairy penguins. They are only one-third as tall as emperor penguins.

Most penguins are black and white, but some, such as king penguins, have flashes of yellow and orange feathers around their necks. Others, including royal and macaroni penguins, have yellow-orange plumes on the tops of their heads.

## POPULAR PENGUINS

**Here are some amazing facts about penguins.**

- **A penguin's feathers grow in thick jumbles —not rows—helping it keep dry and warm.**

- **Huddled together on ice, emperor penguins can survive in temps as low as −76°F (-60°C).**

- **As many as five million Adélie penguins crowd together to lay eggs.**

- **Penguin parents that have lost their eggs might adopt other things—sometimes bits of shell—to care for.**

# Where in the World

Penguins are sea birds. Some kinds spend many months of each year at sea, only heading for land during breeding seasons.

Unlike other penguins, emperor penguins do not ever step foot on land. When they leave the water, they move onto the vast sheets of ice that form when the surface of the sea freezes over. Then they head back to the water to feed.

At the end of every year's breeding season, penguins molt, losing their old feathers and growing new ones. During these one to two weeks when they molt, penguins cannot enter the sea. Without their usually dense

A lone Magellanic penguin checks out a rugged island close to Argentina, South America.

9

On the Galapagos Islands, a pair of Galapagos penguins climb a rocky shore.

coats, the water would wet their skin, overcooling the penguins, which could cause them to become sick and die.

Penguins are found only in the southern half of the world. Several kinds, such as the emperor and Adélie penguins, make their homes around Antarctica. Peruvian and Magellanic penguins live on or near South America. A number of kinds of penguins swim along the coasts and islands of Australia and New Zealand. And jackass penguins live near the tip of South Africa.

The penguins that live the farthest north—near the equator—are named after their home. These Galapagos penguins settle among the Galapagos Islands (near Ecuador, South America), where a cold ocean current from Antarctica cools the water.

## STAYING WARM, KEEPING COOL

Snow does not melt on penguins. Thick layers of fat and dense feather coats help keep body heat in and cold air out. And special blood vessels prevent a penguin's feet from freezing without letting too much heat escape.

If penguins become too hot, they cool off by panting, ruffling their feathers, and shaking their flippers. Penguins that live in warm climates also lose heat through patches of bare skin around their eyes and on their feet.

11

# Water World

No wonder penguins feel at home in the water. Their bodies are built for swimming and diving. Unlike most other birds, penguins have solid—not hollow—bones that make the birds heavier and easier to submerge. Their flippers are strong and flat, like paddles. And their smooth feather coats allow the birds to slip easily through the water. Oil from glands beneath their tails waterproofs the feathers.

Of all birds, penguins are the best swimmers. They fly underwater by using their flippers for power and their webbed feet to steer. Some penguins can suddenly change the direction they are swimming by turning cartwheels.

**A penguin uses its super swimming skills to catch fish.**

**"Flying" underwater, a penguin frequently bursts from the sea to breathe.**

Most penguins can swim up to 6 miles (10 kilometers) per hour, but in bursts, they might move twice that fast. Gentoo penguins are among the quickest swimmers, occasionally reaching 17 miles (27 kilometers) per hour.

As Adélie penguins leave the water, they often pick up enough speed to shoot into the air before landing on their feet. Erect-crested penguins sometimes ride swift waves to shore, then latch onto rocks, so they won't be carried back out to sea.

Penguins are amazing divers. Some kinds make shallow dives and can stay underwater for more than two minutes. Other kinds dive much deeper. Emperor penguins can reach depths of 1,640 feet (500 meters), holding their breath for about twenty minutes. Deep diving makes it possible for them to catch food such as squid.

## CATCHING A BREATH OF AIR

As swimming penguins speed through the ocean, they never stop to breathe. Instead, they surface every few minutes. Surging out of the water with their flippers flapping, they snatch a few quick breaths of air, then plunge right back into the sea.

Leaping in and out of the ocean also serves another purpose. It creates little air bubbles that help the penguins glide more easily—and more swiftly—through the water.

# World Full of Food

Penguins always dine at sea. They gobble up lots of fish and masses of tiny, shrimp-like animals called krill. King and emperor penguins eat a lot of squid, which thrive in the cold waters off Antarctica.

When penguins chase down their dinners, they streamline their sleek bodies as much as possible. They pull their heads down close to their shoulders and hold their feet tightly against their bodies. Then the birds charge through the water, darting this way and that as they nab their prey. Penguins are as nimble as they are quick.

**Sharp beaks and bristly tongues help penguins hold onto slimy food.**

17

Seafood is slippery, so it is a good thing penguins have beaks built for grabbing and holding. Their spiny tongues provide extra grip. Penguins flip the fish they catch, then swallow the prey headfirst and whole.

When penguins have young chicks to feed, they hunt for extra food. Emperor penguins might

**An emperor penguin feeds its chick a soupy meal of fish.**

each stuff themselves with an additional 7 pounds (3 kilograms) of food to take to their newly hatched chicks. Then, they bring up the partly digested meals, and the chicks feed by poking their tiny beaks into their parents' gaping mouths.

If emperor chicks hatch before their mothers return with food to feed them, the father penguins give them "penguin milk." It is not real milk but a mixture of fat and protein. The meal oozes from a tube joining the penguin's throat with his stomach.

## IN THE PINK

Scientists can tell which penguins have been eating plenty of fish and which penguins have been eating mostly krill. The proof is in the color of the waste, or guano (GWA-no), that the birds produce.

Fish eaters tend to leave behind white guano, while krill-feeders excrete pink guano.

Some penguins can eat so much krill that the yolks of their eggs turn a deep pink or even red.

# World of Words

"Yap, grunt, yap, yap," little penguins call to one another. Jackass penguins b-r-a-y like the donkeys they were named after. And around Antarctica, chinstrap penguins chatter loudly.

What is all the noise about? When it is time to breed, most kinds of penguins gather in large crowds. The males, who are the first to arrive at mating places called rookeries, often HONK to claim their breeding or nesting spots.

Male Adélie penguins usually look for nests they have used in other years. When they find the nests, they wave their flippers

**King penguins throng together, trying to attract and call to mates.**

around and holler, "Gug-gug-gug-gug-gaaaaa." That is how they announce, "This is mine!"

When female penguins arrive at a rookery, the males call out to them. Standing tall, the male penguins toss back their heads and belt out "songs." Pairs that have mated before frequently find each other and become

**With beaks open and pointed skyward, chinstrap penguins signal their interest in mating.**

mates again. Other penguins attract new mates.

Two Adélie mates might stand face to face, rocking their heads forward and backward. Then they point their beaks to the sky and cry out. It is their way of saying, "We are together. We are a pair."

Sometimes, penguin sounds are used as alarms. If an Adélie penguin spots danger, such as a hungry leopard seal lurking in the water, it might make a noise that warns others to watch out!

## CRIES IN THE WIND

**Winds howl across the islands where king penguins breed. The noise can make it hard for them to hear and find their mates.**

**King penguins cannot change the pitch of their cries, and they cannot holler louder. Instead, on windy days, they call more often, and they make more sounds in each call— twelve in place of the usual four. Frequent cries have a better chance of being heard during dips in the wind's noise level.**

23

# World of Eggs

Different kinds of penguins choose different places to lay their eggs, such as in caves or burrows. Many penguins prefer to lay eggs right out in the open. Penguins may fight with others to claim their laying spots, then they guard them fiercely.

Some penguins build nests for their eggs. They use whatever material they can find—stones, grass, leaves, or twigs. Royal penguins have even made nests out of bones taken from old penguin skeletons.

Other kinds of penguins build no nests at all. Emperor and king penguins, for instance, simply cradle their eggs on the

**A rockhopper penguin protects two eggs in its nest of grass.**

**Reshuffling its position, a gentoo penguin prepares to settle on an egg.**

tops of their feet. Unlike most penguins, which produce two eggs at a time, emperor and king penguins each lay just one. They tuck it under a thick blanket of belly skin. There it stays warm even in the coldest weather. An emperor or king penguin egg takes about two months to hatch.

Penguin mates work together to care for their eggs. Many males take the first shift, caring for the eggs while the females head back to sea to feed. When the females return to the eggs, the males leave to eat.

While parent penguins are busy tending eggs and protecting them from other sea birds, they survive on nothing but their own body fat. During that time, the penguins can lose more than one-third of their total weight.

## EGGS ON THE ROCKS

**In the Antarctica region, Adélie penguins often nest at the base of rocky slopes or ice cliffs. Resting on their bellies, they scrape out the ground with sharp claws on their feet, then create small "bowls" by piling up pebbles. They try to make sure their piles of pebbles are high enough to keep water out of the nests. Flooding would make the eggs laid inside too cool.**

**If Adélie penguins have trouble finding enough pebbles, they may steal some from others.**

# New World

Peck, peck, peck. Penguin chicks can take three days to break through the shells of their eggs. Then the parent birds warm and protect the chicks, just as they cared for the eggs. Other sea birds—gulls, skuas, and giant petrels—can easily snatch unguarded chicks.

Along the coast of Antarctica, bold sea birds called sheathbills might steal food from penguin chicks. Just as a chinstrap penguin brings up a bit of half-digested krill to feed its chick, a sheathbill can dart between them, scooping up the meal.

**Fluffy and gray, an emperor chick does not look like adult emperor penguins.**

29

**Adélie penguins prepare to take a ride on floating ice.**

As penguin chicks grow, some kinds gather in groups for safety while their parents hunt for food. By the time the chicks have thick, waterproof coats, most are ready to head off on their own. Many kinds of penguins leave when they are only two months old; others, when they are more than a year.

Young penguins do not have to learn how to swim or hunt. They simply plunge into the water and do what comes naturally. They may discover a few enemies in the sea, such as fur seals and killer whales. Around ice sheets near Antarctica, leopard seals are the greatest threat. These fast swimmers skulk in the water, waiting to snap their powerful jaws at Adélie, gentoo, and rockhopper penguins.

Penguins that survive to adulthood will likely live several more years. Chinstrap and yellow-eyed penguins may reach age fifteen or more.

## GO WITH THE FLOE

Penguins do not spend much time at play. But some Adélie penguins seem to take rides for no reason other than just to have fun. Pushing and shoving, they line up to sail on the ice sheets, or ice floes, that drift by.

Leaping onto a passing floe, an Adélie penguin rides along for a short stretch before jumping back to shore. Then it may immediately rejoin the penguin line for a chance to take another ice floe ride.

# Glossary

**Antarctica** — the continent, or land mass, that surrounds the South Pole and is covered with ice.

**breeding seasons** — the times of year when animals gather together and mate to produce young.

**cartwheels** — flipping movements that look like a wheel turning.

**dense** — packed together tightly.

**digested meals** — food that has been changed in the stomach and intestines so that it can be used by the body.

**glands** — parts of the body that take materials from blood and then either remove them from the body or change them to other fluids that can be used by the body.

**guano** — the droppings, excrement, or waste of waterbirds.

**molt** — shed off and get rid of feathers.

**prey** — animals that are hunted by other animals for food.

**rookeries** — breeding or nesting places.

**submerge** — to go underwater.

# Index